MW01201600

For my daughter,
Audrey Julia„
who loves her
bedtime snuggles

Birch Blossom
Books

Watertown, WI

Baby's First Bedtime Prayer

A Lutheran High Contrast Book

By Keely Marie Prekop

Now I lay me down to sleep,

I pray the LORD my soul to keep.

Forgive the sins I've done today.

Thank you for the price Christ paid.

Jesus, guard me through the night,

And wake me with the morning light.

If I should die
before I wake,

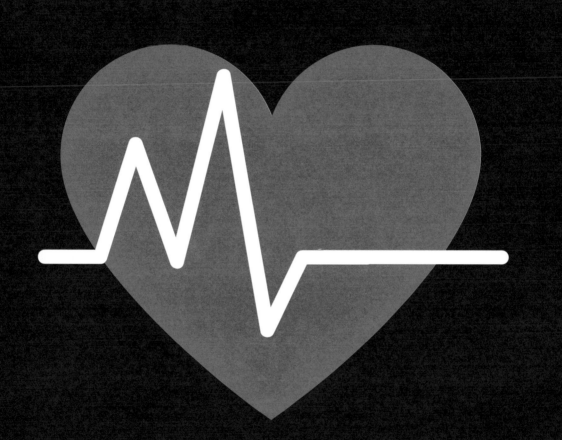

I pray the LORD my soul to take.

If I should live another day,

I pray the Lord would guide my ways.

Amen.

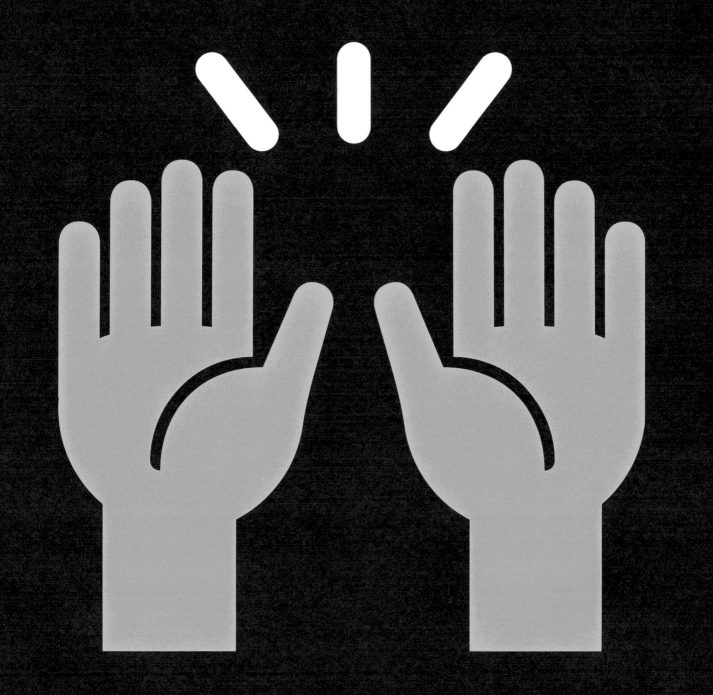

5 Tips for Starting a Bedtime Routine with Young Children

1) Start Small: Take a look at what their current bedtime routine looks like. Don't think you need need an hour long routine to start. Figure out what your family currently does for a bedtime routine and add one thing. We started with brushing teeth. We made sure to brush teeth every night for two weeks. Then we added in cleaning up our toys before brushing teeth. Then we added one story after brushing teeth. Slowly over three months we restructured our bedtime routine to: clean up toys, pajama's, potty/diaper change, brush teeth, bath/shower on bath night, 2-4 stories (each child picks 1 or 2 books), Bible Story, 2 or 3 Jesus songs (each child picks a song and sometimes mom picks one too!), say goodnight, separate goodnight prayer/song with each child in their bed. From start to finish it ranges from 10 minutes to an hour a night. But it all started with picking a time to brush our teeth.

2) Don't give up: Don't let the paragraph above fool you. That list covers every possible combination of what we might get through in a night. We take that list and we are flexible with it. Sometimes its only one song total, sometimes its only the Bible story and no other stories. Sometimes we've sang the same song every night for two and a half months straight. Whatever kind of day you have had, whether it was a 5 songs and 3 stories type of night, or a quick prayer before bed type of night, don't give up on the importance of ending their day with Jesus.

3) Sing, sing, sing: Studies show that children are more receptive to a singing voice than a normal talking voice. Singing creates interest, can slow down words to help children enunciate what they are singing, and pairing singing with actions help children understand more words as they grow older. Make a joyful noise to God! No matter your singing ability!

4) Read short and age appropriate stories: Please do not try to make any child sit through a story above their level. A general rule of thumb is that a child's attention span is the number of their age plus two. My daughter is 2 years old so most likely her attention span is 4 minutes. Whichever Bible story book I pick needs to have colorful pictures to catch her eye and usually shorter than 4 minutes to read. We love The Beginner's Bible series. I was given that Bible as a preschool student and still have my copy. I now give it families in my preschool and use it with my young children at home.

5) Ask Questions: As your children get older, don't be afraid to ask them questions. Point to the pictures and talk about what you see. If you repeat the same story all week, you could ask about what happens in each picture as the child learns the story. Or you can focus on certain vocabulary or special people of the Bible too. Encourage your children to ask questions too! If they ever ask a question that you don't know the answer to, that's okay! Tell them, "You know what Audrey? That is a great question! I don't know. Would you like me to ask/text/email Pastor so we can learn together?" If they say yes, then do it! You both get a chance to grow in your knowledge of God!

Bedtime routines give children a calming way to end their day. It lets them know they are loved, cared for, they know what to expect, and bedtime routines can help with the bedtime blues. When coupled with a family devotion, songs, or prayers, then we are creating a home environment where learning academics, growing faith, and strengthening relationships can all happen at the same time.

Made in United States
Troutdale, OR
01/05/2024

16636833R00017